"How To Invest" series

FIRST-TIME INVESTOR:
GROW AND PROTECT
YOUR MONEY

Paul A. Merriman

with Richard Buck

REGALO
educate - empower

Published by Regalo LLC

ISBN-13: 978-1478206088
ISBN-10: 147820608X

This publication is designed to provide accurate and authoritative information in regard to the subject matter covered. It is sold and otherwise distributed with the understanding that neither the authors nor publisher is engaged in rendering legal, accounting, securities trading or other professional services. If legal advice or other expert assistance is required, the services of a competent professional person should be sought. – *From a Declaration of Principles Jointly Adapted by a Committee of the American Bar Association and a Committee of Publishers and Associations*

To contact Regalo LLC, please email us at info@paulmerriman.com

All profits from the sale of this book – and all books in the "How To Invest" series – are donated to educational non-profit organizations. For more information, visit http://www.PaulMerriman.com

Cover Design by Anne Clark

CONTENTS

ABOUT THE "HOW TO INVEST" SERIES

Paul Merriman's "How To Invest" series provides concise and timeless information for a secure future and stress-free retirement. Each book addresses a specific audience or investor topic. With almost 50 years of experience as a nationally recognized authority on mutual funds and retirement planning, Paul is committed to helping people of all ages and incomes make the most of their investments, with less risk and more peace of mind. All profits from the sale of this series are donated to educational non-profit organizations.

The second book in the series will be: **101 Reasons I Don't Trust Stockbrokers (And You Shouldn't Either)**

For articles, podcasts, updated fund recommendations and more, visit: www.PaulMerriman.com

ACKNOWLEDGEMENTS

Over the years I have learned about investing from many wise people (and a few foolish ones as well), and I am forever indebted to them in more ways than I can say.

I would be negligent if I didn't tell you that you would not have this book in your possession without the patience and wisdom of my wife, Suzanne, and the creative, diligent work of Aysha Griffin and Richard Buck. If this book helps you, then you should be thankful that they are on my team.

INTRODUCTION

I want to congratulate you for taking the first steps toward financial security and freedom in choosing to read this book. As a first-time investor, the knowledge you have, the choices you make, and the habits you establish now, will make an enormous difference in the years ahead.

In this book, I will walk you through the most important steps to build and maintain a successful investment portfolio. In plain language, you will learn exactly what you need to do to set and meet your financial goals. And, after reading this book, you will have the confidence and understanding to know how to make the best financial decisions for the rest of your life.

Planning for the future can be challenging because, when you're young, retirement seems far away and hard to imagine. But I can assure you that it will arrive. You will age. You will want to retire. And if you have a family, you will want to help ensure their future. In addition, you may want to leave a legacy to "give back" to those who have helped you or to support causes in which you believe.

If you invest wisely, you may be able to retire while your friends are still chained to their jobs. That may sound unlikely during these difficult economic times, but it's not magic, and it's not as difficult as you might think.

Regardless of how much money you make, the crucial first step is to put aside a small amount on a consistent basis. You may be 23 and have just landed your first job. Or you may be 40 and have decided to finally get serious about investing. Whatever the case, if you are new to investing, this book is for you.
If you diligently follow the advice you'll find here, you'll have a high probability of enjoying financial independence when your working years are over.

In these pages you will learn:

• How investing really works

• Where you should get your information and place your trust

• How much risk you should take

• How to increase your returns without increasing your risk.

You will also learn about the forces designed to rob you of your hard-earned money and how to avoid becoming the prey of slippery Wall Street salespeople as well as outright crooks and con artists.

Most young investors think the lessons of sound investing don't really matter until they have a lot of money. Many spend a decade or more making unsuitable investments, taking too much risk – or worse, not saving and investing at all.

However, there are at least three reasons why the early years of an investment portfolio are extremely important:

A. The much publicized "magic of compound interest" dictates that every dollar that you invest for 40 years will inevitably be worth much more than a dollar you invest for only 30 years or 20 years.

B. Almost every beginning investor makes mistakes. But I don't believe that they need to be painful or devastating mistakes. You can learn just as much from a $1,000 mistake when you're young as you can from a $50,000 mistake when you're older. And the price of the lesson is much lower.

C. The early years are the time you form the habits and attitudes that separate the most successful investors from those who spend their lives talking about what they could have done, should have done, and would have done differently.

If you do the right things for the first 10 years of your working life, you can easily double your income in retirement.

Of course nothing is guaranteed, and anything is possible.

Win the lottery? It's possible you will win the lottery, and a lot of people who have neglected their finances believe that is their only chance of success. I hope you won't end up like them. In early 2012, the national lottery reached a record jackpot of $640 million. Three people split the pot. As one newspaper headline noted, that lottery produced three winners and more than 100 million losers. Those are not the kind of odds on which you should have to rely.

Give your money to Wall Street? Wall Street brokers are eager to help you make more money. The system is organized so that Wall Street always makes money – and you might or might not. With the knowledge you will find here, you will be far less likely to fall for their sophisticated sales pitches.

As many wise people have said, investing is not a sprint but a marathon. I am not focused on getting good results for you in the next month, the next year or even the next decade. I am focused on the results that you will have for the rest of your life.

If you do the right things from the start, the difference can be huge. And in this book I show you exactly how to do that, and why.

Why should you listen to me? For more than 30 years I have spoken with thousands of investors of all ages and all levels of wealth. I have made it my mission to reach as many people as possible in order to help them be more successful investors. I have taught tens of thousands of people at workshops, written hundreds of articles and several books. I have appeared on national and regional TV and radio, and I've recorded podcasts and DVDs and CDs, all in an effort to teach the sound principles you will find here.

I have now retired from Merriman Inc., the investment firm I founded in 1983. I represent no companies and have no investment products or services to sell you. Both Richard Buck, my co-writer, and I intend to donate all profits from the sale of our books and products to scholarship funds and non-profit educational organizations. I am available to answer your questions and offer many more resources on my website, www.PaulMerriman.com.

So, what do I mean by "huge" differences? I am about to show you some numbers that I hope will get your attention. They show the long-term differences that come from adding just one to six percentage points to your annual return.

In the following table I am assuming that for 40 years you save $5,000 a year, a total of $200,000 out of your pocket, and then you retire. This is theoretical, but it illustrates the point.

Table 1 shows seven annual returns, from 4 percent to 10 percent. The lowest return is what you might expect to get in the long run from an ultra-conservative strategy investing in government bonds and certificates of deposit. The highest return is what you might expect from an all-stock portfolio.

Table 1

Results of 40 years of saving $5,000 annually
at various rates of return

Your investments	Your return	Value after 40 years
$200,000	4%	$475,128
$200,000	5%	$603,999
$200,000	6%	$773,810
$200,000	7%	$998,176
$200,000	8%	$1,295,282
$200,000	9%	$1,689,412
$200,000	10%	$2,292,963

The point of this simple table is that small changes in your annual return can have a huge effect in your results over 40 years. Notice, for example, that by increasing your return from 9 percent to 10 percent, you pick up an additional $603,551. That is three times the total of all the money you saved over the years!

As you read about the various ways to increase your return in seemingly small increments, I hope you'll remember how much **small changes add up over time**.

Your comments and questions are welcome. I can be reached via email at PM@paulmerriman.com

~1~

THE FOUNDATION FOR SUCCESS

1. Be different: Save money regularly.

This is so obvious that I shouldn't have to write it and you shouldn't have to read it. But if you look around and seriously observe your peers, you'll see plenty of people who either don't know this or don't care: **To be an investor, you have to save money**.

Unless you come into a windfall inheritance, if you want to be an investor you will have to save money from your income. You will need to do this every payday, every month, every year. Get in this habit and you're on your way. Ignore this, and the rest of what you read in this book won't matter very much.

2. Be even more different: Live below your means.

I hate to saddle you with two pieces of bad news right off the bat, but you can't follow my first piece of advice unless you spend less than you earn. The good news is that you can make this a habit, and eventually it will become second nature.

Your friends may spend all the money they have and rack up big debts in order to spend even more, all in order to live a lifestyle they can't afford. They will likely wind up with finances so fragile that when a need comes along, they will have to either borrow more money or sell the investments that are supposed to be growing for the long term.

3. Make your money work for you.

There's a terrible trend afoot in the land lately: Many young people, rightly observing the damage to their parents' and grandparents' fortunes from what's being called the Great Recession, have vowed to avoid that fate by shunning stocks and seeking guaranteed returns.

This happened after the stock market's crash of 1929 and also after 1932, 1974 and 1987. After each of these crashes, many investors were unwilling to trust the market again for decades. During those decades, those spooked investors missed out on some of the most productive years in the market.

So my advice to you is simple: Once you have saved money, don't just put it in the bank. Invest it is something that can grow over time. That means owning something – most likely stocks of public companies. When you put money in the bank or buy bonds or anything that's "guaranteed," you are letting your money work for somebody else.

Instead, I want your money to work hard for you, and that means indirectly getting other people to work for you. How can you do this, especially if you have only a small amount of money? That's what this book is about.

4. Treat yourself like a millionaire.

Should you own one stock or many? If you are a savvy investor, more is better. If you own only one stock, you are speculating, betting that you've chosen an Apple instead of an Enron. The majority of individual stocks disappoint their early investors. Many public companies lose money, go out of business or just limp along until some bigger company decides to buy them at a discount.

If you own just one stock, you could lose most or all of your investment. But there's never been a case in which a broadly diversified portfolio of stocks has become worthless. Millionaires invest in 1,000 or more stocks. You should too, using mutual funds.

5. Build your financial future with mutual funds.

Unsophisticated investors buy stocks and bonds one by one, believing this will help them make higher returns. Some think this will help them understand what it means to own a stock or a bond. Others like to follow individual stocks on the Internet. The result, to put it bluntly, is almost always the same: They waste their time and waste an opportunity.

For almost anything you might want to invest in, there's at least one mutual fund that will give you diversification, professional management and recordkeeping.

Some investors shun mutual funds because they don't want to pay the expenses. Here's my answer to that: You'll probably never meet anybody who is more expense-averse than I am. I hate paying even one unnecessary dime in expenses. And virtually all my money is in mutual funds. In my view, mutual funds are the bargain of a lifetime.

6. Make a plan for your future.

Think of investing as a long journey on which you are just setting out. Keep your destination – financial independence – in your mind all the time. You can get there. And when you do, it will be worth everything you had to do along the way.

A goal is a dream with a deadline, and I hope you will dream big dreams.

To see what's possible, study the following table. It shows how much money (in today's dollars) you could have available to spend every year after you retire if you take the right steps now, and keep taking them. Those numbers may seem mighty big, but I believe they are easily within your reach.

7. Imagine 40 years of savvy investing.

The following table takes up where **Table 1** left off.

Table 2
Retirement income resulting from various rates of return

Your annual investment	Your return	Value after 40 years	Your income in first year of retirement
$5,000	4%	$475,128	$19,005
$5,000	5%	$603,999	$24,160
$5,000	6%	$773,810	$30,952
$5,000	7%	$998,176	$39,927
$5,000	8%	$1,295,282	$51,811
$5,000	9%	$1,689,412	$67,576
$5,000	10%	$2,292,963	$91,719

These figures assume you do the following:

A. Invest $5,000 annually from age 25 through 64.

B. Withdraw 4 percent for living expenses when you are 65.

The point of this table is to illustrate the payoff you can have from turning years of savvy investing into cash flow when you retire. Note the enormous differences in your payoff as you achieve higher returns. This is compelling evidence that small increases in return can add up to huge differences in your retirement lifestyle.

8. Learn to recognize the siren song of Wall Street.

Wall Street has a plan for your money, and it involves making money – for businesses and individuals who may or may not be on your side. There's always a salesperson or broker who must be paid as well as some firm that employs the broker. My definition of Wall Street includes the major financial media, as I have described in detail in Chapter 3 of my book "Financial Fitness Forever". You can download this chapter for free when signing up at my website, http://www.PaulMerriman.com.

In the view of Wall Street, if you end up making money, that's fine. But your profits are a far lower priority. Sorry about that.

In addition, I've seen time and again that no matter how you have invested your money, Wall Street always thinks you should do something different; that's how they make money.

You can't be an investor without using the financial industry to some extent. But you don't have to buy high-cost, low-return products. You don't have to take Wall Street's advice. Savvy investors should place their trust elsewhere.

9. Learn to recognize the siren song of Main Street.

Here I'm talking about your friends, relatives, colleagues and neighbors who like telling you about the great investments they have made. Recommendations from friends are great for choosing restaurants, car mechanics and other businesses. But Main Street is not the place to get investment advice.

Your neighbors, relatives and friends are probably not trained in the art and science of investing. They will never show you their full financial records to demonstrate what they are bragging about, and that means you have no way to know whether they are telling you the truth, or whether they've had one success among many failures. Savvy investors should place their trust elsewhere.

10. Learn to appreciate the teachings of the academic community.

There are many college and university professors who study investing. In "Financial Fitness Forever," I refer to them collectively as University Street. They don't want to make a profit from you. They don't care whether you think they're smart. They just want to understand what really works to produce good investing results. Their motive is to impress their colleagues with their research, maybe gain tenure and be published.

Most of what's in this book is based on solid academic research and time-tested results. University Street has found that investors do best when they keep expenses low, diversify widely, accept the returns of the market, pay attention to taxes and much more. Savvy investors place their trust in University Street. I hope you'll be among them.

~2~

BUILDING THE FOUNDATION
FOR LIFE-LONG RETURNS

11. Pay attention to taxes.

As a beginning investor, you are unlikely to be in a high tax bracket. You might think only wealthy people need to worry about taxes. But that would be a mistake. Taxes are inevitable, but you can do a lot about them. In fact, you can eliminate almost 100 percent of any taxes on your investment growth and income.

Later in this book I'll give you some specifics on how to legally reduce your tax liabilities. For now I want to make the point that it really matters what kind of accounts you have. Remember Table 1 and Table 2, which show the hypothetical results of investing over a 40-year period? Those results assume that you achieved your gains without paying taxes on them each year.

If you have to pay taxes as you go, you'll wind up with a lot less money for retirement.

Here's one example: If you achieved a long-term 10 percent return but had to pay taxes of 15 percent on your gains every year, your after-tax return would be only 8.5 percent. After 40 years, that would leave you with only about $1.5 million instead of $2.2 million. (And you would still have taken all the risk of the strategy that produced the pretax 10 percent return.)

12. Pay attention to expenses.

Like taxes, the expenses you pay nibble away at your returns and the gains you will have at retirement. You'll encounter this point again and again in this book, and I hope the message sinks deep inside your mind.

I'm always appalled at how casually investors agree to pay 1 to 1.5 percentage points every year in expenses when they could very easily invest in essentially the same assets for one-tenth that cost. By the time you retire, this difference could easily rob you of $500,000 – more than twice your own total investments over 40 years.

13. Save 10 percent of your income if you can.

Table 1 shows the power of long-term compounding. However, it may be unrealistic in assuming a steady investment of $5,000 every year. When you're 25, you may have a very hard time saving that much. By the time you're 55, you should be able to save a lot more.

In the real world, you'll almost certainly be able to reach your long-term goals if you get in the habit of saving 10 percent of your income each year – and if you invest that money wisely. That means 10 percent out of your own pocket, without counting tax breaks or matching contributions from your employer. The first part, saving, is up to you. The second part, investing wisely, is what you will learn in this book.

14. When you are young, invest in stocks.

When there are decades left before you will need the money you invest, you want that money to grow. No one can guarantee the return you will achieve from investing in stocks (using mutual funds, of course). However, there is little evidence that you will achieve any significant growth if your money is in bonds or certificates of deposit.

It's true that you can reduce your short-term risks by adding cash and bonds to your portfolio. But if you do that, you'll reduce your long-term return in order to gain some short-term comfort. If you're young, that's a poor bargain.

Over the 86 years from 1926 through 2011, long-term government bonds provided a return of 5.7 percent. Meanwhile, the Standard & Poor's 500 Index returned 9.8 percent. That difference is much greater than it seems. Invested in bonds, $1 grew to $118 over that very long period. Invested in stocks, $1 grew to $3,100. Later in this book I'll describe and recommend other types of stocks that did much better.

15. Diversify your investments across many industries.

Many people are tempted to concentrate their investments in a few industries they are sure will outperform the market. In the 1960s, atomic energy and airlines were seen as sure long-term investments. In the 1990s, many investors "knew" that technology companies were so promising that they abandoned common sense and put everything in that sector. I have a friend who knew the banking business very well; just before that whole sector blew up in 2008, he had the majority of his money in the stock of Washington Mutual – and he kept it there while that company imploded and became nearly worthless.

Don't be like these people. If you diversify widely, at any given moment you'll automatically have some of your money invested in whatever part of the economy is going gangbusters. This will happen automatically, and you won't have to worry about it. Savvy investors diversify. You should too.

16. Diversify your investments across many asset classes.

In this book you will learn about a dozen or so important asset classes. An asset class is a group of stocks with similar characteristics, such as large U.S. companies that are popular with investors. (I've just described the asset class known as U.S. large-cap growth stocks.)

At any moment, a few of these asset classes will be leading the market and others will be languishing. Many "experts" on Wall Street and in the financial media will try to convince you they know which of these asset classes will do the best at any given time. But they don't and can't know the unknowable.

I've been paying close attention to these experts for half a century, and I haven't found any whose predictions reliably pan out. My best advice is the same as in Item 15: Diversify.

17. Diversify your investments geographically.

The majority of the world's stock market capital lies beyond the borders of the United States. In spite of that well-known fact, you would be surprised how many U.S. investors believe all they need are companies based in their own country. Many advisors encourage their clients to have most or all of their stock investments in U.S. companies, which are familiar and comfortable. All the research of which I am aware indicates that long-term investors have benefited from splitting their stock investments between U.S. and international funds. Sometimes international stocks do better than domestic stocks, and sometimes U.S. stocks lead the way. Often they move up and down together, but sometimes their gains and losses offset each other, reducing volatility (risk).

There's a whole world of opportunity waiting for you, and you should take advantage of it. Based on historical returns and many years of working with clients and their portfolios, I recommend that you split your stock investments 50/50 between companies based in the United States and ones based in other countries. Over long periods, that combination increases return and reduces volatility.

18. Start thinking about retirement now.

This may seem strange advice for somebody who may be 30 or 40 years away from retirement, but I think it's important. Think of it as advance planning on steroids.

By the time you invest your first dollars toward retirement, you should have at least a rough idea of how much money you'll need to accumulate, and you should have chosen a distribution strategy.

For example you may determine that (in today's dollars) you will need $80,000 a year to live on and that you can expect half of that from Social Security. That means your portfolio will need to "pay you" $40,000 a year for as long as you live. Using a conservative 4 percent distribution assumption, that suggests you should have at least $1 million in your portfolio when it comes time to retire.

Table 3
Total lifetime results of various rates of return

The following table takes the set of calculations from Tables 1 and 2 a step further, showing the potential results of various rates of return during your life and after your life is over.

Your invest-ments	Your pre-retirement return	Your retirement return	Your total withdrawals	Left for your heirs at your death	Grand total	Every $1 you invested became
$200,000	4%	4%	$557,121	$452,843	$1,009,964	$5.05
$200,000	5%	5%	$815,507	$767,100	$1,582,607	$7.91
$200,000	6%	6%	$1,209,551	$1,306,012	$2,515,563	$12.58
$200,000	7%	7%	$1,815,681	$2,232,839	$4,048,520	$20.24
$200,000	8%	8%	$2,755,274	$3,830,134	$6,585,408	$32.93
$200,000	9%	8%	$3,593,652	$4,995,572	$8,589,224	$42.95
$200,000	10%	8%	$4,877,503	$6,780,266	$11,657,769	$58.29

Each increment in the table results from a change of just one percentage point in annual return. Unsophisticated investors often regard a mere one percentage point as being insignificant, but this table shows how wrong that is.

Table 3 assumes that an investor achieves a single return for 40 years of accumulations and continues that return through 30 years of retirement distributions. There are two exceptions: Investors who received 9 percent returns before they retired and those who received 10 percent. I don't think it is realistic to project such high returns, which entail unnecessary levels of risk, through 30 years of retirement. Therefore, I have assumed that retirees will achieve no more than 8 percent during the last 30 years.

~3~

TAKING RISKS

19. Lose money.

Yes, you read that correctly. I'm telling you to lose some money in your investments. This is an extremely easy one for you to do. In fact, I guarantee that you will lose money as an investor if you take the risks I'm advocating in this book.

This isn't a bad thing. It's a natural and normal part of being invested, and you should embrace it. In my book "Financial Fitness Forever" I defined risk as: a possibility that you invite into your life knowing that you could lose something important.

Losing money is a good thing only if you recover your losses. And you can do that only if you stay in the market, as I advise. However, if you let your emotions start to dictate your investments and you sell, you will be locking in your losses. I hope you won't do that.

20. Profit from losing money.

Again, that means what it says. It's another example of how the most successful investors benefit from taking a counter-intuitive view of things. Another way to summarize this point: Celebrate bear markets, and take advantage of them.

The age-old formula for making money is to buy low and sell high. A bear market drives prices down, making it easier to "buy low." That's what you want to do, especially when you are a beginning investor with lots of time ahead of you.

When the market goes south or stagnates, ordinary investors get nervous and run the other way. In the first dozen years of this century, the U.S. stock market was essentially stalled, at least as measured by the Standard & Poor's 500 Index. (In contrast, diversified portfolios similar to what I'm recommending here rose about 7 percent a year, outperforming over 95 percent of investors' actual portfolios.)

Millions of investors moved their money out of stocks and into bonds seeking safety (even though interest rates were sinking to the lowest levels on record).

No! No! No! These are exactly the times that savvy long-term investors should look forward to so they can buy more shares for every dollar they invest. To do this, you have to have faith in the long-term future of capitalism. However, I don't think you'd be reading this book unless you had that faith.

So, my bottom-line advice is to put your dollars to work and take advantage of the market misery experienced by other investors. In the long run, when you buy shares at lower prices, you turn that short-term misery into your long-term gain.

21. Figure out your tolerance for risk.

There are many ways to figure out how much risk you should take in your portfolio. I recommend you start by determining the return you will need in order to meet your goals. Then look at historical data to determine what would have been a low-risk way to achieve those goals. You will find some helpful data in the next two items in this book.

You will probably be tempted to check some of the many online risk-assessment tools that will ask you some questions and then prescribe an asset allocation for a proper amount of risk. One that may be helpful to you is from Vanguard: (https://personal.vanguard.com/us/FundsInvQuestionnaire)

The problem is that these tools can't really know you, and you will have a hard time knowing the right answers. Whatever answers you give will likely be plugged into a large database, and you will get a "canned" recommendation that might or might not be suitable for you.

Whatever results you get, you must take them with a grain of salt. Quite often the questions in an online test will fail to uncover something very important about you, and that failure might give you results that will not serve you well. Garbage in, garbage out.

22. Consider one portfolio for the rest of your life.

Lots of things in life are much more fun than assessing your risk tolerance. Some people want to go through this process only once, then forget it and move on. I totally understand that.

Based on everything I know about the past, I believe most people can meet their long-term goals if they invest 60 percent of their money for growth – that means stock funds – and 40 percent for income, which means bond funds.

The 60 percent gives your money plenty of power to take advantage of the good times in the stock market – historically about two of every three years. And the 40 percent will help smooth out the bumps along the way, making it much easier for you to stay the course.

Here's the evidence: From 1951 through 2011, this strategy produced a higher return than the Standard & Poor's 500 Index – at about one-half the risk.

23. Fine-tune the level of risk in your lifetime portfolio.

The 60 percent equity portfolio I just described has an expected long-term return of 7.5 to 9.5 percent. In a severe bear market, you should be prepared for a one-year loss of 30 to 35 percent with this asset allocation.

If you choose a different equity allocation, your expected returns and losses will change accordingly. The following table shows what I expect from several other combinations.

Table 4
Expected returns and risks

Equities	Bonds	Expected return	One-year expected loss
50%	50%	7% to 9%	25% to 30%
60%	40%	7.5% to 9.5%	30% to 35%
70%	30%	8% to 10%	35% to 40%
80%	20%	8.5% to 10.5%	40% to 45%
90%	10%	9% to 11%	45% to 50%
100%	0%	9.5% to 11.5%	more than 50%

All these projections are based on the assumption that you follow my recommendations for diversification in equity funds and bond funds.

24. Understand the implications of your choice.

When you're looking at ways to reduce your investment risk, it's easy to want to dial down your exposure to the volatile stock market. What's wrong, after all, with the concept of safety?

But before you take stocks out of your portfolio and replace them with bonds, make sure you understand the tradeoff. As a general rule, for every additional 10 percent that you hold in bonds, you can expect your long-term rate of return to be reduced by 0.5 percent.

Some popular asset-allocation formulas prescribe a heavy commitment to bonds for young investors. I think this is a mistake. For example, consider the "advice" that an investor at the age of 30 should have 30 percent of his or her portfolio in bonds. That reduces the long-term expected return of that portfolio by 1.5 percentage points.

For a 30-year-old, that is a very high price to pay for "safety" which is of little or no value at that age. I'm not telling you what to do here, just telling you to think carefully about what your decision could mean over the long term.

I'll now present three alternate asset allocation approaches that could indicate how much you should invest in stocks and how much in bonds. They aren't perfect, but each has its merits.

25. Consider the simplest of formulas.

A popular formula suggests you subtract your age from 100 and invest that percentage in stock funds, with the rest in bonds. That means that at age 25 you would hold 75 percent in stocks and 25 percent in bonds. The best I can say about this approach is that it's mechanical and easy to understand, and that it reflects the idea that most people's risk tolerance declines as they age.

However, as noted above, this does a big disservice to young people, who need growth much more than they need safety. This formula makes pretty good sense for people from 50 to 70, but outside those ranges I think it's too simplistic.

If you choose this formula for your own investments, use 120 instead of 100 in the formula, giving you an extra shot of equity exposure through your investing lifetime.

26. Consider my own age-based formula.

Here's a very simple formula that will put you at least in the ballpark. Until you're 35, invest 100 percent in stocks. At age 35, move 15 percent of your portfolio into bond funds.

Every five years after that, move 5 percent of your portfolio out of stocks and into bonds. This will give you a 70/30 portfolio (70 percent in stocks and 30 percent in bonds) at age 50 and a 55/45 portfolio at age 65. The majority of investors can invest successfully with these allocations.

27. If you're really spooked by stocks, make sure you can't lose everything.

A few years ago I met a nervous young investor who had good savings habits and a high-paying technology job. I was startled to learn that for years he had been investing 20 percent of his portfolio in bond funds.

I told him I couldn't believe that 20 percent in bonds was enough to keep him from losing a lot of money in a severe bear market. He agreed that it wasn't. He told me that during the stock market's crash in 2007 and 2008, those bond funds kept him in the game because he knew he couldn't lose everything he had set aside for his future.

If something like that will keep you in the game when the going gets rough, then it's definitely worth your consideration.

28. Know when it's time for a change.

Very few of us have static lives that, once set in motion, stay on the courses that we initially plot for ourselves. We get married. We get divorced or widowed. We have kids or adopt kids. We change careers or jobs. We move to a different city, a different state or a different country. We go back to school. We go back to work. Our health changes. We get older. We retire. We get fired, or we're wiped out by legal troubles. We come into an unexpected pot of money.

Each one of these events has the potential to change our goals and our risk tolerance. And each may require us to re-think our investment strategies.

It can be hard to know when events like this require a change and when they don't. Whenever you experience some sort of major life event, I suggest you consult a financial advisor (one who does not have products to sell) who can help you look objectively at the question: Is it time for a change in strategies?

~4~

HOW TO SELECT THE BEST ASSET CLASSES

29. Put the right kinds of assets into your portfolio.

Imagine that you are making a stew to feed your family. Your first decisions are to choose the ingredients that will go into it. This choice will have a huge impact on the quality of your final product. Likewise, your choice of asset classes will have a huge impact on the quality – as well as the long-term performance – of your portfolio.

A term you should know is "asset class." This phrase might sound intimidating, but it's fairly simple: It refers to a group of assets (either stocks or bonds)_that have similar characteristics. To return to the analogy of making a stew, you might think of vegetables as one class of ingredients and spices as another.

Selecting the right asset classes is the most important thing you will do as an investor, second only to the basic decision to save some of your money instead of spending all of it.

In this section you will learn about the asset classes I recommend. Each has an extensive history of enhancing the long-term performance of investment portfolios. Think of this section, if you like, as the list of ingredients that will go into your stew. Later, we will talk about how to make sure you have the right amount of each asset class in your portfolio.

30. Concentrate first on equities.

Equity asset classes are pieces of the stock market, if you will. Bond investments are very important too, and I'll discuss them later. But you should first make sure you get the equities side of the portfolio right.

Equity asset classes make up at least half – and usually more – of a typical long-term investment portfolio. Investors who are 35 or younger should probably have all their retirement funds in equities.

Equities provide the power to make your money grow over time. When Boeing designs an airplane, it pays enormous attention to the jet engines that will get the plane into the air and safely to its destination. Everything depends on those engines. Likewise in your portfolio, everything will depend on the equities that you choose.

31. Understand the importance of size.

When I describe equity asset classes, I'm going to rely on some industry jargon: large-cap, mid-cap and small-cap. In order to follow along, you'll need to get this concept clearly in mind. These terms refer to the average size of companies in a portfolio.

A large-cap company is one that's worth a lot of money in the stock market. Some prominent examples include Microsoft, Google and General Electric. Capitalization refers to the theoretical total value of a company – its total shares outstanding times the current market price.

Imagine a company that has two billion shares of stock outstanding. If each share is worth $75, that company has a total capitalization of $150 billion. In relative terms, that qualifies as a large-cap company.

Now think of another company, also with two billion shares outstanding. If those shares trade on the stock market for only $1 each, that can be described as a small-cap company, with a total capitalization of $2 billion. Mid-cap companies, or mid-cap stocks, fall somewhere in between.

32. Understand why size matters.

Large-cap companies and small-cap companies are parts of an overall stock market, and their price trends usually move in the same direction. But they move at different speeds, and this can be to your advantage.

The best illustration I've ever seen of this is found in the following graphic: "History of the Size Effect." It shows how, over short periods and sometimes over extensive periods, small-cap stocks and large-cap stocks can move very differently.

History of the Size Effect

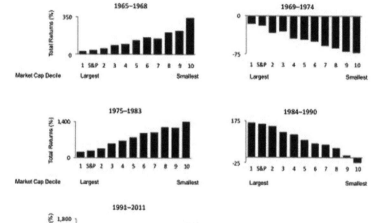

- The size effect can persist for long periods in either direction.
- These long periods can immediately be succeeded by a reversal in the opposite direction.

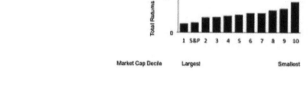

This graphic was created by Dimensional Fund Advisors and is reproduced here with permission. For an explanation of what these bar graphs show, check out the article on my web site: http://paulmerriman.com/why-company-size-matters/.

As you can see, at any given time, either large-cap stocks or small-cap stocks will be leading the way in the market. You can never tell in advance which will do better, but I think your best bet is to own them 50/50 and periodically rebalance. If you do that, you should expect a higher return and lower risk than if you owned only U.S. stocks.

33. Understand value vs. growth.

Another basic concept to understand is the difference between a "value stock" and a "growth stock." There's a chapter in my book "Financial Fitness Forever" that provides a detailed explanation of this difference. Here I offer an abbreviated version of it.

A **growth stock** is one that is popular with investors for various reasons. The company may be in a glamorous industry. It may have a track record of always reporting higher sales and higher profits. Its business may appear to be easy to understand. Because this company is so popular, investors are willing to pay a premium to own its stock. This is very nice, but if investors suddenly change their collective minds about the company, this premium can vanish quickly.

A **value stock** is one that, for whatever reason, is not particularly popular. Uncertain about its future, investors are unwilling to pay a premium price for its stock.

Value stocks can be regarded as the bargains of the stock market. Sometimes, as you know, a "bargain" like this may not even be worth the asking price and it might remain unloved for a long time. But many times, today's ugly ducklings turn into tomorrow's swans.

Here's why this matters: Over long periods of time, value stocks have consistently performed better than growth stocks. As a result, long-term investors usually benefit from having a healthy chunk of their portfolios in value stocks.

One other term you'll see in my discussion of equity asset classes: **Blend**. This refers to a mutual fund portfolio that does not exclude either growth stocks or value stocks. A blend fund includes both. A good example is the asset class known as U.S. large-cap blend stocks.

34. Own U.S. large-cap blend funds.

If you've followed the discussion above, you know that a U.S. large-cap blend fund owns large U.S. companies including both growth and value. This is a very basic asset class, typified by the **Standard & Poor's 500 Index**. This index is the benchmark most commonly used to measure the U.S. stock market; it is made up of about 500 of the largest companies headquartered in this country.

I think the best way to invest in this asset class is to buy an index fund. The **Vanguard 500 Index** is hard to beat for this. For more on recommended funds, visit my website.

For each of the other asset classes I recommend, I'll compare its long-term return to the return of the Standard & Poor's 500 Index.

Long-term returns

Time range	U.S. large-cap blend	S&P 500 Index
1926-2011	9.3%	9.3%

35. Be picky about your other asset class choices.

A good chef is very picky about what goes into the stew. I'm very particular about what goes into my portfolio, and I hope you'll take the same attitude toward yours.

The asset classes I'm about to recommend are all in my own portfolio. To get there, they had to pass two tough tests. First, they had to have a long-term track record of outperforming the Standard & Poor's 500 Index. Second, they had to show they can reduce risk by being non-correlated (i.e., don't go up and down together) with that index.

36. Own U.S. large-cap value funds.

It's true that the large-cap blend funds I recommend include **value stocks**. But because value stocks have been so productive over the long term, I want you to have more of them than you would get with just a blend fund.

A 100 percent value fund will give you more of an asset class that is likely to outperform both growth funds and blend funds over time. By recommending that you own a blend fund (growth and value) plus a value fund, I'm telling you to over-weight your assets toward value – without abandoning growth stocks.

The best way to own value stocks is through an index fund. A fine example is the **Vanguard Value Index Fund**.

Long-term returns

Time range	U.S. large-cap value	S&P 500 Index
1926-2011	10.4%	9.3%

37. Own U.S. small-cap funds.

As noted above, small-cap stocks often grow rapidly in value, and I want you to own some of them through one or more mutual funds. To use an example that is very familiar in my hometown of Seattle, the young Microsoft of 1986 could (and did) grow much, much faster than the much larger Microsoft at the end of the 20th century and the first decade of the 21st.

It's not hard to find small-cap blend funds such as the **Vanguard Small-Cap Index Fund.**

Long-term returns

Time range	U.S. small-cap	S&P 500 Index
1926-2011	11.7%	9.3%

38. Own U.S. small-cap value funds.

Over long periods of time, value stocks have outperformed growth stocks by a huge margin, and small-cap stocks have outperformed large ones by a meaningful margin. The logical next step, as you might guess, is to combine small and value. And it turns out that small-cap value stocks have been exceptionally productive.

Individually, such stocks are exceptionally risky. But when you own them by the hundreds, as you can in a small-cap value fund, they can be very rewarding as one ingredient in a balanced portfolio.

Again, I recommend using an index fund such as the **Vanguard Small-Cap Value Index Fund.**

Long-term returns

Time range	U.S. small-cap value	S&P 500 Index
1926-2011	14.4%	9.3%

39. Invest in real estate funds.

Just so we're clear at the outset, this does <u>not</u> mean your home.

Real estate has taken a beating the past few years, but funds that own commercial properties like apartment complexes, malls, parking lots and office buildings have a long track record of producing good returns.

Often such properties are owned by real estate investment trusts (REITS). I recommend you include a REIT fund in your portfolio. The best way to do this is with an index fund such as the **Vanguard REIT Index Fund**. Because of the way that the tax laws treat REITs, these funds belong in your IRA and your 401(k), but not in a taxable account.

We don't have data going back to 1926, but we have enough data to establish a long-term pattern.

Note that the date ranges of returns in the following asset class comparisons are not all the same, depending on the data available.

Long-term returns

Time range	U.S. REITs	S&P 500 Index
1978-2011	12.4%	11.3%

40. Use international asset classes to put the world to work for you.

I recommend you invest half your equity portfolio in international funds, mirroring the U.S. equity asset classes I have outlined.

The broad up-and-down movements of international stocks are usually in synch with the trends of the U.S. stock market. But U.S. and international stocks go up and down at different rates, and occasionally with different timing when the currencies of various countries go up and down relative to the U.S. dollar. This makes the two groups a good pair for smart diversification.

Just as important, more than half the world's investment capital is headquartered outside the United States. You should own some of it.

41. Invest in international large-cap blend and international value stocks.

International large-cap blend funds are easy to find. Almost every 401(k) and similar retirement plan has at least one. International value funds are not quite so common, but if you have one available you should use it.

Long-term returns

Time range	International large-cap blend	S&P 500 Index
1970-2011	8.9%	9.8%

Time range	International value	S&P 500 Index
1975-2011	14.7%	11.5%

42. Invest in international small-cap funds.

The attractive characteristics of small-cap stocks are just as relevant outside the U.S. borders as within them.

As in your U.S. equity portfolio, choose an international small-cap blend fund and, if you can find an international small-cap value fund, you should include that too.

Long-term returns

Time range	International small-cap blend	S&P 500 Index
1970-2011	14.3%	9.8%

Time range	International small-cap value	S&P 500 Index
1982-2011	13.8%	11.0%

43. Invest in international real estate funds.

International commercial real estate is attractive throughout the world, and fortunately you can get in on this asset class through mutual funds. One of the best is the **Vanguard Global ex-U.S. Real Estate Index Fund**. Although this asset class has a limited history that can be tracked, I have no reason to believe it will disappoint investors in the future.

44. Invest in emerging markets funds.

This is an asset class without a direct U.S. counterpart. Emerging markets are countries whose economies have especially high growth potential. **Vanguard's Emerging Markets Stock Index**

Fund tracks equity returns in 21 countries, including Brazil, Russia, India and China.

While the stocks of such countries are more volatile than those of Europe and the United States, they also have provided superior long-term returns. In the long run, they should give your portfolio a boost.

Long-term returns

Time range	Emerging Markets Index	S&P 500 Index
1988-2011	12.5%	9.5%

45. Skip large-cap growth funds.

If you own a large-cap blend fund, you'll have plenty of the largest growth stocks. As noted above, value stocks have outperformed growth stocks over long periods of time.

My recommendations include stocks, and they weight the allocation toward value. This applies to international funds as well as U.S. funds.

Long-term returns

Time range	U.S. large-cap growth	S&P 500 Index
1926-2011	8.5%	9.3%

Time range	International large-cap growth	S&P 500 Index
1975-2011	8.5%	11.5%

46. Don't invest in mid-cap stock funds.

The portfolio I'm describing relies on what I call smart diversification, letting you mix several asset classes together to achieve a higher return, at less risk, than the average return of those asset classes.

Smart diversification requires assets that behave differently from one another. Mid-cap stocks typically don't behave radically differently from either large-cap stocks or small-cap stocks.

Mid-caps are typically right in the middle. Their returns are better than those of large-cap funds, but less than small-cap funds.

In my view, the best way to diversify is to invest at the ends of the size spectrum, then rebalance annually, instead of investing in the middle. To see at a glance why this makes sense, look back at the bar graphs above in Item # 32.

47. Don't invest in technology funds.

If you own large-cap and small-cap blend funds, you'll own enough technology stocks to benefit when they periodically soar to new heights. Funds that put most or all of their money in technology stocks, even index funds that follow the NASDAQ Index, are about twice as risky as the Standard & Poor's 500 Index, yet they have delivered lower returns.

Even though some high-profile technology stocks like Google and Apple have achieved spectacular growth, technology stocks as an asset class (which is what we are concerned about here) have not been worth the risks. In bear markets, the NASDAQ Index has been a very scary place to have your money.

Long-term returns

Time range	NASDAQ Index	S&P 500 Index
1972-2011	8.1%	9.8%

48. Don't go for the gold.

Gold has attracted a compelling myth: It will protect you from inflation, from world crises – in fact, from whatever disaster might await you. Gold's proponents can always point to short periods when the metal has dramatically outperformed nearly everything else. But I want you to be a long-term investor with a long-term outlook.

Focus on the reality of gold, not the myth. When you look at the facts, they are clear. The price of gold was fixed by the government until 1971. Since then, it has failed to match the stock market, let alone outperform it.

Gold may glitter, but that doesn't make it a good investment. Here's my advice: Put gold in your jewelry box if you like, but leave it out of your portfolio.

Long-term returns

Time range	Gold	S&P 500 Index
1972-2011	8.3%	9.9%

49. Don't invest in commodities.

The story here is very similar to gold. Many experts say the world is running out of natural resources, which can only go up in value. I don't disagree, but that doesn't make commodities a good investment. Commodities don't pay dividends, and they don't pay interest.

A few years go some of my colleagues at Merriman Inc. studied this issue and found that, after expenses, the expected return of commodity funds was less than that of ultra-safe Treasury bills.

If you own the asset classes that I recommend, you'll have plenty of exposure to energy, basic materials and other industries that stand to benefit directly from commodity inflation.

The numbers tell a story. The Dow Jones Commodity Index, which tracks prices starting in 1982, had a compound rate of return of 5.6 percent through 2011. In that same period, the **worst** return of any of the nine equity asset classes I recommend was 8.9 percent (international large-cap stocks).

Long-term returns

Time range	Commodities	S&P 500 Index
1982-2011	5.6%	11.0%

50. Use the following table to keep these equity class recommendations straight.

Table 5

Putting this all together, these are my recommendations, along with a blank column that you can use for your own investment choices:

Asset class	Recommended %	Your %
U.S. large blend	11%	
U.S. large value	11%	
U.S. small blend	11%	
U.S. small value	12%	
U.S. real estate	5%	
International large blend	9%	
International large value	9%	
International small blend	9%	
International small value	9%	
International real estate	5%	
Emerging markets	9%	
Total	**100%**	**100%**

~5~

UNDERSTAND MUTUAL FUNDS

51. Give yourself an elementary education in mutual funds.

Numerous places in this book, I've recommended mutual funds for your portfolio, and I name specific ones for specific purposes. You could simply take this advice without understanding what you're doing. But I think that would be a mistake.

In this section I'll cover some basic factors that distinguish mutual funds from one another. This isn't difficult material, and you will understand much more thoroughly and powerfully the world of mutual fund investing.

For more on this topic, I recommend the book "Mutual Funds For Dummies" by Eric Tyson as well as my own upcoming title in this series focused specifically on mutual funds. (To be notified of new title releases, please register at my website).

52. Choose no-load funds and save a bundle.

This is one of the most important distinctions you will learn among mutual funds. A load fund is one for which you pay a sales commission in one form or another. A no-load fund is one you can acquire without a sales commission.

The difference – made by a 5 percent sales load on an equity fund – is very big, roughly 0.5 percentage points in annual return. Unless you need the services of a broker to help you choose funds – and you won't need that after you read this book – the load you pay gives you absolutely no benefit. None.

You can learn lots more about this in Eric Tyson's book. But the bottom line of my advice is pretty simple: Unless it's labeled as a no-load fund, don't invest in it.

53. Choose passively managed funds instead of actively managed ones.

One of the biggest mistakes investors make, including everyone from amateurs to professionals, is trying to beat the market by buying and selling. There's a whole chapter on this in "Financial Fitness Forever," and I hope you'll read it if you are even slightly intrigued by the notion that you can find a fund manager who knows how to beat the crowd.

Only a minority of actively managed funds beat popular benchmarks such as the Standard & Poor's 500 Index. And data going back decades shows, year after year, that most investors in actively managed funds do not even obtain the returns that those funds advertise.

Along the way, actively managed funds saddle their shareholders with false hopes, higher expenses, higher taxes (at least in taxable accounts) and higher portfolio turnover.

Passively managed index funds, by contrast, usually have very low expenses and relatively low turnover. They almost always track their benchmark indexes very closely, so shareholders know what they are getting. The best place for your money is in these passively managed funds.

54. Invest in broadly diversified funds.

You can buy sector funds, which invest in narrow slices of the market such as technology or energy or medicine. But these give you no advantage and only increase your level of risk. A blend fund, either large-cap or small-cap, will give you all the exposure you need to the important industries in which you should invest.

Similarly, you can invest in concentrated funds, sometimes known as "focus" funds that hold relatively few stocks, often only 20 to 40. These funds rely on the ability of a manager to pick "winners" in the stock market. I've been studying mutual funds for many decades, and I've never found a mutual fund manager who could successfully produce superior long-term returns in this manner.

55. Choose funds with low portfolio turnover.

The portfolio turnover of a mutual fund is a statistic that's readily available at Morningstar.com. Basically, it measures the percentage of a fund's assets that are bought and sold each year. Some funds have turnover as low as 6 or 7 percent. Some have turnover of 300 percent or more.

John Bogle, the founder of Vanguard and the inventor of index funds, has a rule of thumb that every 100 percent in portfolio turnover costs shareholders one percentage point of return.

High turnover hurts you in several ways. For one, it drives up expenses, because every purchase and sale costs something, and those costs are passed through to shareholders. For another, high turnover suggests that a manager is taking a short-term view of the market.

If you own a mutual fund in a taxable account, high turnover hurts you in a third way: It drives up your tax bill. Every sale potentially involves a capital gain, and you are the one who will have to pay the taxes on that gain.

56. Choose a mutual fund family (or a few families) wisely.

"Family" in this instance means a company that sponsors and manages mutual funds under a common name. Vanguard, T. Rowe Price, Fidelity and American Funds are examples of large fund families.

Every fund family has certain characteristics. Vanguard is known for very low expenses. American Funds offers only load funds (so I don't recommend this family). Some fund families specialize in a certain kind of investing; Dodge & Cox and Third Avenue, for example, focus on value funds.

If you can find all the asset classes you need in one fund family, limiting yourself to that family will make your investments convenient. You'll get a single regular statement so you can see your portfolio as a unit, which is a good way to look at it. And rebalancing among funds will be easy if they're all within one family.

On the other hand, there's no reason you have to limit yourself to one fund family if you find a particularly compelling fund somewhere else. You will have to weigh the tradeoff between convenience and the merits of whatever fund you're considering. Now let's look at three large fund families.

57. Consider investing in Vanguard funds.

My favorite fund family for investors who don't use advisors is Vanguard. Here are three reasons.

First, Vanguard is the king of index funds, which I recommend highly. Vanguard also has low-cost actively managed funds that are worth considering in market niches not covered by index funds.

Second, Vanguard funds have very low expenses and very low turnover. For taxable accounts, the company has some top-tier tax-managed funds. Portfolio turnover is low in these funds, and you can get every asset class you need in a no-load Vanguard fund.

Third (this is something that few people realize), Vanguard is owned by the mutual funds it operates. That means that the company is owned by the shareholders of those funds, an arrangement similar to that of a credit union.

For many years, I've been recommending specific Vanguard funds for long-term investors. These recommendations have been independently tracked by The Hulbert Financial Digest newsletter.

For the 10 years ending March 31, 2012, my all-equity Vanguard portfolio returned 7.4 percent, compared with 4.1 percent for the Standard & Poor's 500 Index. My moderate Vanguard portfolio, with 60 percent in equities and 40 percent in bonds, returned 7.5 percent.

You can find my Vanguard portfolios in the **Appendix** of this book. I also recommend you check my website for updates: http://paulmerriman.com/pauls-mutual-fund-and-etf-recommendations/

58. If your retirement plan uses Fidelity funds, make the most of them.

Fidelity is one of the largest mutual fund companies and the 800-pound gorilla offering employee retirement plans. The company's advertising is everywhere, boasting about its team of analysts who are familiar with investing around the world. This is valuable to investors in actively managed funds, but I don't think it's much benefit to those who take my advice and choose index funds.

Fidelity's most attractive offerings, in my view, are a few large, ultra-low-cost index funds. The company operates many 401(k) and similar retirement plans. That is the main reason that I include recommended portfolios of Fidelity funds.

Fidelity's funds tend to have higher expenses and higher portfolio turnover than Vanguard's. Beyond that, there's nothing really wrong with this fund family. But if you have a choice, I would recommend Vanguard.

For many years, I've been recommending specific Fidelity funds for long-term investors. These recommendations have been independently tracked by The Hulbert Financial Digest.

For the 10 years ending March 31, 2012, my all-equity Fidelity portfolio returned 5.8 percent, compared with 4.1 percent for the Standard & Poor's 500 Index. My moderate Fidelity portfolio, with 60 percent in equities and 40 percent in bonds, returned 6.3 percent.

You can find my Fidelity portfolios in the Appendix and also online at the same link referenced in #57.

59. If your retirement plan uses T. Rowe Price funds, make the most of them.

T. Rowe Price operates many 401(k) and similar retirement plans. Its fund lineup isn't as extensive as that of either Fidelity or Vanguard. But this company takes a conservative approach to just about everything it does. Its expenses tend to be higher than those at Vanguard but may be lower than those at Fidelity.

If you follow my recommendations, I don't think you'll go very far wrong at T. Rowe Price. Nevertheless, I think you are likely to get a better ratio of return to reward – in other words, you'll get more units of return for every unit of risk you assume – at Vanguard.

You can find my T. Rowe Price portfolios in the Appendix and also online at the same link referenced in #57.

60. If you have $100,000 or more, consider investing in Dimensional Fund Advisors funds.

Not very many first-time investors have the $100,000 or more needed to qualify to open an advisory account that will give them access to DFA funds. But if and when you can, I strongly recommend you invest in this family of low-cost no-load funds, which were created for large institutional investors.

The only individuals who can invest in DFA funds are clients of registered investment advisors who pass the scrutiny of DFA, a company that was founded and is managed by some of the most impressive academics with whom I'm familiar.

DFA funds compare favorably with Vanguard funds, and you'll find a detailed discussion of that in my book "Financial Fitness Forever." In short, they have ultra-low expenses and turnover combined with ultra-high diversification. Although they are not strictly index funds, DFA funds track the asset classes I recommend, often doing a better job than even index funds.

61. Understand the basics of exchange-traded funds (ETFs).

ETFs are a relatively new arrival among investment products. They are very much like mutual funds, offering a variety of portfolios in most of the important asset classes. Their expenses are usually low, and their portfolio turnover varies as much as the turnover of mutual funds.

The big difference is this: The price of a mutual fund is set only once a day, based on closing prices of the assets in its portfolio. Investors buy shares from the fund company, and the fund company buys them back when investors are ready to sell.

ETFs, by contrast, trade on stock exchanges and in the over-the-counter market throughout each day, like stocks. The price of an ETF changes from moment to moment whenever the market is open.

Unlike mutual funds, ETFs do not have minimum initial investment requirements. This makes them valuable for investors who want wide diversification even when they have very little money.

Because buying and selling ETFs can involve trading costs, I prefer mutual funds. In addition, their constant availability may be too tempting for investors who tend to react to the market's ups and downs throughout a trading day.

You can find my ETF portfolios in the Appendix and also online at http://paulmerriman.com/pauls-mutual-fund-and-etf-recommendations/.

62. Don't bother with target-date retirement funds.

Most of the major fund families offer one-size-fits-all funds that are designed to be a simple solution to risk control, based on only one bit of knowledge about each investor: that investor's expected retirement date.

For instance, the Fidelity Freedom 2030 Fund is aimed at people who expect to retire (hence the "Freedom" in the name) in the year 2030. If for some reason you are determined to put all your money in a single fund, and if you will turn 65 in the year 2030, this is supposedly the right choice for you. Or so the marketing departments of fund companies would have you believe.

This concept has many problems. I'll mention four.

Problem 1: You can't know in advance just when you will retire, so how do you choose between Fidelity Freedom 2030 or Fidelity Freedom 2035? Furthermore, retirement usually isn't like turning off a light switch. More and more people are retiring gradually, which makes choosing a date a bit murky.

Problem 2: Target-date retirement funds are mass-market products designed to appeal to investors' desire for comfort. Accordingly, their portfolios are heavy on large-cap U.S. stocks and very skimpy on small-cap stocks, value stocks, international stocks and real estate.

Problem 3: One of the biggest appeals of these funds is the notion that they provide the proper amount of risk for their shareholders. But that would be true only if everybody who planned to retire in a given year had the same risk tolerance. That's not the case at all. If you're smart enough to read this far in this book, then you are plenty smart enough to figure out a more customized solution for yourself.

Problem 4: These funds usually allocate too much of their portfolios to bond funds for young investors. Typically a fund designed for 25-year-olds will hold 10 percent of its assets in bonds. I see no justification for that choice, which may cost shareholders 0.5 percentage points in annual return without providing enough cushion to be meaningful in a bear market.

63. Hit the bulls-eye with a target-date fund.

This is another paradox, particularly right after I've told you not to bother with target-date funds. Investing, like life, is riddled with paradoxes, because not everything is cut and dried.

I know that some people simply can't apply all the recommendations I'm making in this book. Doing so takes thought and introspection. It takes time and requires you to assume responsibility for consistent action. In addition, the market has a way of testing investors emotionally day after day, week after week, year after year. It can seem overwhelming.

If all this is just too much for you, a well-chosen target-date retirement fund may be the best decision you can make. You'll have a manager making the decisions, your asset allocation will probably put you on the low to moderate part of the risk scale, and you won't have to think about all the things I'm outlining.

Note the phrase "well-chosen" above. Not all target-date funds are created equal, and the differences can mean tens of thousands of dollars to the value of your portfolio when you retire. You can learn about these differences in Eric Tyson's book, "Mutual Funds for Dummies."

~6~

STUFF HAPPENS: EMERGENCIES

64. Create an emergency fund.

No matter what your age or circumstances, unexpected things can and will happen to you. Savvy investors accept this and plan for it. An entire book would be needed to cover all the possible variations of creating an emergency fund. However, a few key points will get you heading in the right direction.

Some people's lives, for whatever reason, seem to be filled with emergencies. They need a large cash cushion so they won't have to go into debt or prematurely liquidate their long-term investments. Other people seem to handle life's ups and downs without major financial strain. Wherever you fall on that spectrum, you should have some pool of money you can get your hands on quickly when you need to.

How much? I don't have a simple, easy answer. As a beginning investor, you need to have the bulk of your money working for you over the long term. As a person who lives in the real world, you need some reserves.

Minor emergencies (you must define that for yourself) can often be handled using a credit card. But for anything that you can't pay off in three or four months, you should have a stash of cash.

Here's a quick-and-dirty approach: If you are truly just starting out, I suggest you divert 10 percent of the money you're investing for retirement and put it into an emergency fund. This will build up over time, and after a few years you may be able to reduce that percentage or stop contributing altogether.

If you accumulate an emergency reserve equal to three months of your living expenses, it is probably sufficient.

65. Invest your emergency funds conservatively.

You can find opinions all over the map about where to invest emergency money, and nobody can tell you in advance where you'll get the optimum combination of return and safety. The problem is that you don't know if this will be short-term money or long-term money, because you don't know when (or even if) you will need to tap into it.

Some people will tell you to keep it in an ultra-safe money-market account. That way, every dime you set aside will be available whenever you want it. Others will tell you to invest in a short-term bond fund, which will at least pay a bit of interest. As I'm writing this in mid-2012, the Vanguard Prime Money Market Fund pays almost nothing: 0.03%. The Vanguard Short Term Investment Grade Bond Fund has a current yield of 2.6%.

My friend and colleague Richard Buck keeps his family's emergency money in a balanced fund that invests in both stocks and bonds. His reasoning is that he's not likely to tap into this often, and he wants potential growth.

A mutual fund I sometimes recommend for emergency savings is the **Vanguard Wellesley Income Fund.**

~7~

NO-NOS: DO NOT DO THESE THINGS

66. Do not use short-term products for long-term money.

Bank certificates of deposit, Treasury bills and money-market funds are great places to keep cash reserves and money you may need in the relatively near future. But as a beginning investor, you are probably looking at decades before you plan to withdraw your money.

Your bank would love to have you keep a lot of money in your checking and savings accounts. But you won't earn much that way. A recent mailing from a credit union disclosed the interest rate it pays on "high-yield" checking-account balances over $50,000: 0.25%. That's right, one quarter of 1 percent. If you kept $100,000 in your checking account, the "top" $50,000 in your account would earn the whopping sum of $125 a year.

The bank deposit may seem safe, especially with a federal FDIC guarantee. But that rate of interest won't even preserve your money's purchasing power in light of inflation, much less give you a long-term return.

67. Just say no to insurance products like variable annuities.

You'll find a detailed treatment of variable annuities in my book "Financial Fitness Forever." If you are in the highest tax bracket and you've used up all your other options and you have lots of money you may not ever need, then maybe, just maybe, this could be a worthwhile product for you.

Here are five reasons you should *not* invest with these products:

1. You will pay very high expenses.
2. The "tax advantages" that are used to sell these products are counterproductive to most people – and in fact are much worse than most investors understand.
3. Variable annuities require you to buy life insurance whether or not you want or need it.
4. Redemption fees can make it extremely expensive to change your mind.
5. Insurance contracts are typically long and cleverly written, giving almost all the "protection" to the insurance company and relatively little to the customer.

68. Don't load up on your company's stock.

If your employer offers to sell you company stock in your 401(k) plan, it may seem tempting. But it can be a trap. You may think you are an ideal investor in your company's stock because you understand the business, the industry, the products and the competition.

That lure is very seductive. But I have seen company stock come back to bite far too many otherwise-savvy investors who were blindsided by events they could not foresee.

If you are already counting on your employer for income and benefits, that's enough dependence on one entity. Prudent investors place their future in the hands of hundreds and even thousands of companies. You should too.

69. Don't borrow from your 401(k) or similar retirement plan.

Your retirement plan may seem like a good source of "emergency savings," but it's not. Many plans restrict or prohibit withdrawals from current employees, so you might not be able to do this even if you want and need to.

The rules regarding 401(k) loans can be harsh. Here's one example: If you have an outstanding 401(k) loan and you leave your job for any reason before the loan is repaid, the entire amount is due immediately – at a time when you are least likely to be able to pay it back.

Here's a second example: The interest you pay on the loan will be payable to yourself – but because of the way the rules are written, you will be taxed twice on that interest: once before you pay it to your 401(k) account and again when you eventually withdraw it.

70. Don't choose your investments based on a newsletter.

If you're like most young investors, you will be tempted to get aggressive and take unnecessary risks in hopes of "making a killing" to jumpstart your investment life. Part of the investment industry is always eager to help with promises of riches. I wish it weren't true, but unfortunately the only people likely to get rich are those who sell the newsletters, not those who follow their advice.

Three decades of following many newsletters has convinced me that most of their implied promises are simply untrue. Their claims of expertise in the market are mostly fantasies. The returns they tout are usually fiction.

However, hope is such a strong, undying emotion among investors that the newsletter business can be very lucrative. I know of investment newsletters that take in $5 million or more every year, even though their recommendations have lousy track records.

Newsletter publishers have the privilege of the First Amendment to make whatever claims they wish to make without the necessity to offer evidence. Fortunately, you have the privilege of just ignoring them, and I strongly advise you to exercise that privilege.

In sum, buying a newsletter is like paying a sales load.

71. Just say no to market timing.

This is a strange recommendation coming from me, because I believe in timing and I have about half my own money invested using mechanical (that's an important qualifier) strategies designed to get your money out of the market during the worst down periods and back in during the best of the good periods.
If I have a lot of money invested this way, why would I tell you not to do it? The answer is because I am retired, and capital preservation is much more important to me than it should be to a first-time investor.

A first-time investor should embrace down markets as a chance to buy assets at bargain prices. If you agree with that, then market timing is counter-productive.

72. Don't go into debt to invest.

As I write this, interest rates are ridiculously low, and it can seem tempting to take out a personal loan at 3 or 4 percent and use the proceeds to invest in things that might pay you two or three times that much over the long haul.

But whatever you invest in could lose much of its value without giving you much warning. Yet the loan you take out will still be there, and the lender will expect to be paid.

Many people think they can jump-start their investments using "OPM," or other people's money. In doing so, they greatly increase their level of risk.

I'll say it again: If you're smart enough to benefit from this book, then you're smart enough to follow this basic principle: Invest only with money that you own.

73. Don't say no if your parents offer to help you get started.

Here's an interesting exception to the point I just made. If you are just starting out in a career and don't have much spare income, find out if your parents would loan you $5,000 a year so you can fund a Roth IRA. If you did that for 10 years, and then started to repay the loans, you would be miles ahead in your retirement than if you waited 10 years to start investing.

To briefly spell out the terms of such an arrangement, here is an example of what you might do. When you're 24 and need most or all of your income for immediate needs, borrow $5,000 and invest it in your IRA. Pay your folks interest on it every year. Then when you are 34, pay back the first $5,000 you borrowed, using money you would otherwise use to invest in an IRA. You'll have a decade of earnings behind you, and your parents will collect some reasonable rate of interest. Keep doing this for nine more years. This could be one of the most powerful gifts they ever give you.

74. Don't try to beat the market.

This is the broader lesson behind my earlier advice to choose passive funds instead of actively managed funds.

If you are determined to try to beat the market, several outcomes are very predictable and probable:

~ Your mind will be focused on short-term trends instead of long-term returns.

~ You will likely place a lot more trust in Wall Street and Main Street than you should.

~ You will pay unnecessarily high expenses and fees.

~ You may pay unnecessarily high taxes, thus prematurely removing money from your portfolio.

~ You will take more risk than is needed to achieve the return you need.

~ You will not diversify properly since you will come to "know" that you have figured out the market.

~ You will waste a lot of time and emotional energy needlessly focusing on your investments.

75. Learn WHY you should forget about beating the market.

Many financial advisors follow a study that's been continuing since the 1980s, done by a research firm in Boston named DALBAR, Inc. DALBAR compared the reported returns of mutual funds with the average returns of actual shareholders.

The results were very startling. During the 20 calendar years ending in December 2011, the average investor in U.S. equity funds achieved a return of 3.5 percent. During that same period, the Standard & Poor's 500 Index had an annualized return of 7.8 percent.

There are two main reasons for this. First, people made in-and-out timing decisions, thinking they were helping themselves when it turned out they were doing the opposite. Second, investors must pay to invest, and the average investor pays too much in expenses and sales commissions.

Numerous academic studies have found the same general result. You may think that your investment savvy makes you an exception, but millions of people before you have sustained huge losses in that belief.

76. Use index funds to match the market and meet your goals.

Once you are willing to "resign yourself" to not beating the market, I think you deserve to celebrate your smarts. If you can get the returns of the market indexes, you will be statistically ahead of the majority of your fellow investors. You can think of this as being "above average" because you accept the market averages.

In all my years of talking with beginning investors, it has been rare to meet someone who had to beat the market in order to achieve his or her financial needs in retirement.

In contrast, I have talked to hundreds of intelligent and dedicated people who tried to get ahead by outsmarting the market. Unfortunately, the vast majority of them fell far behind the returns of the low-cost index funds they scorned. Many were forced to work longer or scale back their dreams for retirement. This is particularly sad because they could have easily taken care of their needs by following the advice in this book.

~8~

THINK ABOUT TAXES

77. Make good use of tax shelters.

You may be in a relatively low marginal tax bracket, but you should not neglect the effect of taxes on your investment portfolio. Like expenses, taxes are a burden to be minimized or avoided altogether when you can.

Every dollar you pay in taxes is a dollar that can't work for your long-term benefit. That means you not only lose that dollar, you lose all the money that dollar could earn for you over a lifetime.

Wall Street has created many products designed to appeal to tax-averse investors. Some of those products – like the two I describe in this section – are very valuable. (Actually, the federal government created these two products.)

Others, such as the variable annuities I described earlier, are designed more to create benefits for Wall Street than for investors.

Unless you are in a very high tax bracket or have very unusual circumstances, I hope you will be wary of sales pitches that purport to cut your tax bill.

However, the Individual Retirement Arrangement, universally known as the IRA, and the 401(k), or similar retirement plan you may have through your employer, are tools I hope you will use.

78. Get the most from your employee retirement plan.

If a 401(k) or similar plan is available where you work, sign up for it immediately if you have not already done so. You will get a tax deduction for money you set aside from your pay. In many plans, employers offer an incentive for participating by matching part or all of your contributions. This is an offer that's too good to pass up, as it amounts to a form of "free money" that you would not receive otherwise.

Each employer determines the investment choices offered in its own plan. Very few plans offer all the equity asset classes I recommend, but that should not stop you from contributing.

79. Use my recommendations in your 401(k) step-by-step.

There's little chance that your company plan will let you invest in all my recommended asset classes. But with a methodical approach, you can make that plan work for you.

Fundamentally, what you want is low-cost diversification. You can achieve the low-cost part of this by choosing funds with the lowest expense ratios (and, of course, make sure that you aren't paying a sales load).

The diversification comes from focusing first on the most important diversifiers: size and value. Here's how: For starters, it will be easy in almost all plans to choose a large-cap U.S. fund and a large-cap international fund.

Then look for a U.S. small-cap fund and a U.S. value fund. Even if that's all you have, it's a great start. Next look for an international small-cap fund, an international value fund and an emerging markets fund.

After you have secured those asset classes, add (if you can) U.S. and international small-cap value funds and U.S. and international real estate funds.

If you can't get all these in your plan, don't worry about it. When you have other money to invest, you can fill in the gaps in other accounts.

80. Fund your IRA.

The IRA is a staple of savvy investors. It has solid benefits and few drawbacks.

In an IRA, you choose a mutual fund company or brokerage firm, then invest in almost anything you choose.

You may contribute up to $5,000 a year ($6,000 if you are 50 or older). In most cases, you have to wait until you're 59½ years old to withdraw the money without paying a 10 percent penalty to the IRS.

There are two main types of IRAs. If your income is within certain limits, your contributions to a **traditional IRA** are tax-deductible. When you withdraw the money, presumably in retirement, you will be taxed on your withdrawals. However, your investment income stays in your account without taxation until you withdraw the money. Also, by the time you retire there's a good chance you will be in a lower tax bracket than when you were employed, thus resulting in lower taxes paid on your withdrawals.

Your contributions to a **Roth IRA** must be made with money on which you've already paid taxes. But the silver lining in this arrangement is that you will not be taxed when you take out the money.

(Although you can contribute to a traditional IRA and a Roth IRA, your total contributions for any tax year cannot exceed the $5,000 or $6,000 limit mentioned above.)

81. Choose your IRA type carefully.

If you have a high income or a complex tax situation, you may benefit from consulting a Certified Public Accountant (CPA) to help you choose between a Roth and a traditional IRA. (You can have both.)

While the two are mathematically equal in the long run, the Roth IRA's tax-free earnings have a psychological edge. For a beginning investor, I'm inclined to recommend the Roth IRA over the traditional.

82. Choose your IRA custodian carefully.

Every IRA has what's known as a custodian, usually a brokerage firm or a mutual fund company. When you contribute money, you send it to your custodian; when you eventually withdraw money, you receive it from your custodian. In addition, your custodian keeps records for you, makes reports to the IRS when necessary, and carries out your instructions for making investments.

Your choice of custodian will determine the options you have among asset classes and how much you pay in fees.

My first-choice recommendation for an IRA custodian is Vanguard. You can use Vanguard's excellent fund lineup and at the same time use its brokerage subsidiary if you need to supplement Vanguard funds. Vanguard's fees are among the lowest you'll find, and its service is excellent.

~9~

FIXED-INCOME ASSET CLASSES

83. Know when to use bond funds.

As stated earlier in this book, if you have many years to go before you expect to withdraw from your portfolio, you may not have much need for fixed-income funds (which I will refer to here as bond funds). Bond funds can provide a stabilizing agent to the long-term diversified equity portfolios I recommend. Their expected long-term return is lower than that of stock funds, along with much less volatility.

I don't have a foolproof formula for how much of your portfolio should be in bonds and how much in equities. In general, as you get closer to the time you'll need your money you will have more desire for stability and less time for long-term growth.

Because this book is designed for beginning investors, I'll assume that you need only a quick overview of some of the major points of this topic, described below.

84. Understand the relationship between bond prices and interest rates.

Bond prices respond to changes in interest rates. Think of the relationship between bond prices and interest rates as a teeter-totter: When one end goes up or down, the other end always moves in the opposite direction. Think of interest rates as one end of this piece of playground equipment and bond prices as the other end.

• When interest rates rise, the prices of existing bonds go down. The reason is simple: If you own a $1,000 bond that pays 5 percent, you get $50 a year in interest. If interest rates go to 10 percent, giving investors $100 a year, nobody will pay you the full price for your 5 percent bond. For purposes of income, your bond is now worth $500 in the market. (If you hang onto it, however, you'll still get the full $1,000 at maturity.)

• When interest rates fall, just the opposite happens, boosting the market value of older bonds with higher interest rates.

If you pay attention to financial trends, you'll frequently hear references to expected changes in interest rates. If you keep the teeter-totter image in your mind, you'll be able to instantly grasp one of the most predictable effects of such changes.

85. Understand two other reasons you could own bonds.

Beyond stabilizing a long-term portfolio that contains equities, there are two other reasons people might own bonds.

Some people, mostly retirees, own bonds in order to receive the interest they pay. Typical corporate bonds pay interest every six months, but bond funds that own dozens or hundreds of issues pay interest monthly. If the interest you receive is enough to meet your income needs, then bonds can be a good, reliable source of that income.

Some people own bonds in the hope that they can make a profit by buying low and selling high. If you understand the teeter-totter relationship I just described, you can easily see how that works. You can buy bonds at relatively low prices when interest rates are high. Conversely you can sell bonds at relatively high prices when interest rates are low.

This strategy requires great patience, and I am not advocating it. Interest rates have been relatively low for a long time and, as I am writing this in 2012, it's hard to imagine rates falling much farther. Experts have been predicting higher interest rates for years, and I am certain that rates will someday go back up. But I have no idea when that will be.

86. Understand safety differences among types of bonds.

Because I recommend bonds in order to mitigate risk in your portfolio, I think you should use relatively safe bonds. That's why I recommend U.S. government bonds, which are widely regarded as the safest in the world. From 1926 through 2011, long-term corporate bonds returned 6 percent; long-term government bonds returned 5.7 percent.

Government bonds typically pay lower interest than corporate ones, mainly because that interest is considered more reliable.

Among corporate bonds, safety varies from "blue-chip" issues by the biggest and most well-established corporations to "high-yield" bonds issued by companies with lower credit and less-certain prospects.

To cite a real example, Microsoft can raise the money it needs without offering high interest rates, because the probability of repayment is extremely high. By contrast, Ford Motor Co. has a low credit rating because it's in an industry facing severe challenges. As a result Ford has to pay higher interest rates on its bonds.

Bonds of companies with low credit ratings are not a good source of stability and safety in your portfolio.

87. Understand short-term bonds vs. long-term bonds.

A bond is essentially an IOU, a promise to repay a loan at some fixed time in the future, usually with regular interest payments in the meantime.

Imagine that you are ready to loan me some money, and I give you two options. First option: I will pay you back after one year. Second option: I will pay you back in 20 years.

You will quickly figure out that the 20-year option is much riskier than the one-year option. You will require me to pay more interest if you loan me money for 20 years rather than if you choose the shorter term.

That's the way it works in the bond market. Long-term bonds are regarded as more risky than short-term ones. Investors demand higher interest rates on long-term bonds, which gives those bonds higher yields.

88. Skip international bond funds.

If you own bond funds in order to reduce volatility, international bonds will not do what you want. These funds go up and down – not only with changes in interest rates but also with changes in the relative value of various currencies; this gives them much more volatility than their U.S. counterparts.

The most productive international bond funds from the most recent 10 years were emerging markets bond funds. But their volatility was like that of equities – making them ineffective at reducing overall volatility.

~10~

BRING THE RIGHT FRIENDS TO YOUR INVESTMENT PARTY

89. Cop an attitude.

After working with thousands of investors over many years, my colleagues and I identified some important traits that differentiate the most successful investors from the others. Entirely aside from how much money they have and what they invest in, the best investors share certain common attitudes. (These are described in more detail in Chapter 11 of "Financial Fitness Forever.")

While you can't control what happens in the market or the world, you can control what you "bring to the party" inside your mind. The next several items can make a huge difference to your ultimate success as an investor.

90. Be willing to trust.

Trust is tricky. I don't want you to trust Wall Street or Main Street. As noted above, I want you to trust history and academic research. But here I'm talking about something more basic. Investing money requires a leap of faith: faith that the market will continue to reward savvy long-term investors, and faith that you will have a future that is worth looking forward to.

Neither I nor anybody else can prove that the future will reward you for doing the right things. But you should do them anyway. Cultivate the attitudes and habits that have helped thousands of investors get through the inevitable tough times.

91. Bounce back when you're knocked down.

I don't have many guarantees, but one of them is this: If you invest directly or indirectly in the stock market, you will lose money. I also guarantee that your investments won't always turn out the way you want or expect. Curveballs are inevitable. When they come along, unsuccessful investors often give up, turning what could be temporary losses into permanent ones.

When you learned to walk, you stumbled and fell again and again – and you kept trying until you got it right. You'll need to do this as an investor, and now – when you're starting out – is the best time to get used to that notion. Winston Churchill, whose whole life was peppered with serious setbacks, said it this way: "No matter what, never give up."

92. Keep your perspective.

The most successful investors I've known are those who can keep their cool in bear markets, bull markets, and events that seem to spell political, economic or social doom. Bad things have been happening for thousands of years, and this is not going to change. Still, the world has survived famines, wars, dictatorships, plagues and ignorance, to name just a few.

Successful investors can tell the difference between what's important and what's not. They know the things they can control (their investment choices, their expenses, their asset allocation), and they don't waste much time on things that they can't control, such as what the market is going to do tomorrow, next week, next month or next year.

To help you develop and keep a healthy perspective for long-term investment success, I suggest you read the article, 10 Retirement Lessons from the Smartest People I Know, on my website at http://paulmerriman.com/articles/ten-retirement-lessons-from-the-smartest-people-i-know/

93. Be patient.

Here's another guarantee: If you are investing money that you won't need for decades, I promise that your balance next week or next quarter or next year won't make much difference in the long run. If you continually focus on short-term results, you'll undermine yourself again and again. Regard time as your ally, because – especially as a beginning investor – it may be the greatest resource you have.

Can you remember what was happening in the market exactly one year ago? Whatever it was, I'm certain that the commentators and pundits and other experts made it sound really, really important. But if you can't even remember it, was it really that momentous?

94. Don't throw away your common sense.

Wall Street hopes you'll believe you can have your cake and eat it too. They hope you'll go for overpriced financial products that seem to combine guaranteed gains and risk-free investing.

If there were an investment that offered that combination, your common sense should tell you that Wall Street's full-time money managers of Wall Street would not leave the rewards for individual investors like you and me. No way! Instead, billions of institutional dollars would instantly flow into such investments.

Your common sense should tell you that if big professional investors don't want to put their money into something that seems perfect, there's a good reason why. That should tell you to stay away.

95. Get in the habit.

Equally important to your long-term success are the things you do routinely – your habits. I cannot over-state how important it is that you repeatedly do the right things without having to think about them every time. Two good habits that we've already described are saving money and living within your income, or delaying gratification.

The next few items cover some other useful habits you should form now.

96. Know where you are going.

The most successful investors I have known always have a destination in mind. They have measurable goals to keep tabs on how they are doing. Investing for your future is akin to setting out on a long road trip. You can follow your nose in whatever direction interests you, and it might (or might not) be rewarding. But if there's a specific place you really want to go, this casual approach won't get you there (except maybe by accident).

Don't build your financial future like that. Instead, get in the habit of always having clearly articulated and measurable goals. Then you can be like the traveler with a road map and a destination. Suddenly, you'll know what to do. And if you get off track, you'll know how to get back.

97. Make a plan.

Even with a road map in hand, you won't automatically get to your destination in an efficient way. Successful investors make a habit of making plans to achieve their goals. In most cases you will need to periodically review and modify your plans to keep you in synch with your changing needs, the changing circumstances of the markets and your evolving knowledge.

Your plan can be elaborate or simple, depending on what works for you. If it's too elaborate, you might procrastinate using it or updating it. If it's too simple, it might not be very useful. If you have trouble with this, consider getting a professional advisor – somebody who doesn't sell products – to help you.

98. Control your emotions.

It's been said many times that Wall Street is driven largely by greed and fear. These emotions come from necessary desires. You wouldn't be an investor if you didn't want to make some money in one form or another. But when that desire runs amok, it turns into greed. We've all seen it far too many times: Unchecked, greed can override common sense, knowledge and even the best-laid plans.

Likewise, one of the most important things you need to do as an investor is limit your risk and avoid major losses. Yet when your legitimate concerns for safety get out of hand, caution can turn into fear, and fear can turn into panic, leading you to make poor decisions with potentially unfortunate consequences.

Entire books have been written on this topic, but my next two points will hit the highlights.

99. Don't get greedy.

I could make a convincing case that greed has been the ruin of more successful investors – and businesspeople for that matter – than any other single factor. In the late 1990s, the U.S. stock market was on a tear, led by technology and telecommunications companies. Stocks were going up so fast that many people abandoned diversification and put everything into tech stocks and funds. Some investors were so sure of themselves that they borrowed money on their credit cards, expecting to "at least" double their money every year or two.

Just after the turn of the century, the whole stock market tumbled in a severe bear market that ruined the future for many investors who could have met their goals without taking undue risks.

Market bubbles have always been temporary, and they tend to burst quickly and unexpectedly. If you know what return you need to meet your long-term goals, don't try to hop on a market bandwagon to exceed that return.

100. Don't be spooked by fear.

In 2008 and the first part of 2009, the financial news was truly awful; fear ran rampant. Many investors bailed out of the market, abandoning their carefully constructed strategies and locking in the losses they had experienced. Then, to the surprise of almost everybody, the market made a stunning recovery in late 2009 and 2010. The frightened investors who had sold everything didn't get the benefit of one of the most favorable short-term rallies in recent history.

Markets go up and down, and losses are normal. Have you carefully controlled your exposure to risk? Are you many years away from needing the money you have invested? If your answers are yes, you will hurt yourself more than help yourself by reacting to short-term bear markets.

~11~

Will You Be A Successful Investor?

101. At least once a year, give yourself a reality check.

After you have taken my recommendations for putting together your portfolio, and after you have lived with it for a while, you may not have much more that needs to be done – other than, of course, continuing to add money.

To help you avoid getting bogged down by boredom, I've created a little self-test to help you see if you are really on track. This isn't hard, as there are only nine topics. Your honest answers to the following questions will tell you whether or not you are really on track with a winning strategy that's right for you.

A. **Are you confident that you can stay the course and follow your plan no matter what happens in the markets?**
You will probably answer "yes" to this, being proud of the decisions and choices you have made. And that of course is the right answer. But keeping coming back to this, and watch your actual behavior.

If you don't actually stay the course, you may have taken too much risk.

B. **Are you happy to wait patiently for the extra return you expect from your superior long-term strategy?**

Again, the "right" answer is yes, and that's the attitude with which you will probably start out. But monitor yourself for feelings and especially for actions. Impatience has been the ruin of many investors who have implemented – and then unraveled—their carefully crafted plans.

C. **Do you have the courage to "just say no" to Wall Street's sales pitches?**

It can take many years, even decades, for investors to finally shake off the notion that somebody on Wall Street has found some special way to make lots of money with low risk. The most successful investors I have known have eventually realized that, despite all the sales pitches, there is no magic on Wall Street.

You'll be far better off if you accept this sooner instead of later.

D. **Is there long-term evidence and academic support for the benefits of your strategy?**

If you follow my recommendations, the answer will be yes. But keep coming back to this one whenever you are tempted to give in to fads and fears of the moment.

E. **Are you willing to let go of worry over what you can't control?**

This is extremely hard for some investors, especially in this day of 24/7 investment media that want to keep all of us on the edge of our chairs.

If you want to worry about the uncontrollable as a form of entertainment, I suppose that you have a right to do it. But as far as I'm concerned, you should not exercise that right until after you have done everything you can do to control the things that you actually CAN control.

F. **Are you immune to the latest fads and the latest returns?**

Again, the answer should be yes. I promise you there will always be some investment that's been doing spectacularly well lately, whether that means recent days, recent weeks, recent months or even recent years.

However, if you follow my advice to diversify very broadly and carefully, you'll have much more than a few years or months of evidence on your side. You'll have more than two centuries.

G. Can you explain your strategy to somebody else easily and succinctly?

This is a tough test, but it's a very good one. You don't have to be able to explain every detail. But if you can give a reasonably convincing argument to somebody who's not an expert, perhaps your mother, you will know your strategy is strong.

If you don't know why you're doing what you're doing, it will be easy for somebody from Wall Street or Main Street to plant doubts in your mind that may make you stray from your deliberate course. But if you're firmly grounded, you can much more easily deal with the sales pitches and arguments that would lead you astray.

H. Does your strategy protect you from making big mistakes?

It should. The key issue here is whether you will actually follow that strategy. A decision that may seem inconsequential can wind up having life-changing effects.

I. Are you diversified enough?

You're on the right track here if no single thing has to happen for you to be successful – and no single thing is likely to derail you. That's worth thinking about, and if you can answer "yes" to this question, then you are on the right track.

APPENDIX

PAUL MERRIMAN'S MODEL MUTUAL FUND PORTFOLIOS

I believe millions of mutual fund investors fail to get the full benefits available to them at the mutual fund families they use. If they understood and used their choices better, they could make more money without taking more risk.

In my books and podcasts and workshops over the years, I have provided the knowledge that investors need in order to make the best fund choices. In the suggested portfolios that follow, I show exactly how to put that knowledge to work at three of the largest mutual fund families in the United States.

Whether you are picking among options in a retirement account managed by one of these companies or shopping for funds in an IRA or a taxable account that you manage, the following tables will show you how to gain access to the most important asset classes.

In each case you will find aggressive, moderate and conservative recommendations for using the choices available at Vanguard, Fidelity, and T. Rowe Price.

VANGUARD MODEL PORTFOLIO
SUGGESTED ALLOCATIONS

Fund	Aggressive	Moderate	Conservative
500 Index	10%	6%	4%
Value Index	10%	6%	4%
Small Cap Index	10%	6%	4%
Small Cap Value Index	10%	6%	4%
REIT Index	10%	6%	4%
Developed Markets Index	10%	6%	4%
International Value	20%	12%	8%
FTSE All-World ex-U.S. Small Cap Index	10%	6%	4%
Emerging Markets Stock Index	10%	6%	4%
Intermediate-Term Treasury	0%	20%	30%
Short-Term Treasury	0%	12%	18%
Inflation-Protected Securities	0%	8%	12%

FIDELITY MODEL PORTFOLIO
SUGGESTED ALLOCATIONS

Fund	Aggressive	Moderate	Conservative
Spartan 500 Index	11%	6%	4%
Large Cap Value Enhanced Index	11%	7%	5%
Small Cap Enhanced Index	11%	7%	4%
Small Cap Value	12%	7%	5%
Real Estate Investment	5%	3%	2%
Spartan International Index	9%	6%	3%
International Value	18%	10%	7%
International Small Cap Opp	9%	5%	4%
Emerging Markets	9%	6%	4%
International Real Estate	5%	3%	2%
Intermediate Government Income	0%	20%	30%
Spartan S/T Tr Bond Index	0%	12%	18%
Inflation-Protected Bond	0%	8%	12%

T. ROWE PRICE MODEL PORTFOLIO
SUGGESTED ALLOCATIONS

Fund	Aggressive	Moderate	Conservative
Equity Index 500	10%	6%	4%
Value	10%	6%	4%
Small-Cap Stock	10%	6%	4%
Small-Cap Value	10%	6%	4%
Real Estate	10%	6%	4%
International Equity Index	10%	6%	4%
International Growth & Income	20%	12%	8%
International Discovery	10%	6%	4%
Emerging Markets Stock	10%	6%	4%
U.S. Treasury Intermediate	0%	20%	30%
Short-Term Bond	0%	12%	18%
Inflation Protected Bond	0%	8%	12%

Exchange Traded Funds Tax-Deferred Portfolios

The following portfolio is composed of my picks for the best ETFs anywhere, representing every asset class I recommend. These funds are available commission-free at discount brokerage houses, including Charles Schwab. ETFs can be especially attractive to first-time investors, as they require no minimum investment.

Fund	Symbol	Aggressive	Moderate	Conservative
Schwab U.S. Large Cap	SCHX	11%	6%	4%
Vanguard Value	VTV	11%	7%	5%
Schwab U.S. Small Cap	SCHA	11%	6%	4%
Vanguard Small Cap Value	VBR	12%	7%	5%
Vanguard REIT Index	VNQ	5%	3%	2%
Schwab International Equity	SCHF	9%	5%	3%
iShares MSCI EAFE Value Index	EFV	9%	6%	4%
Vanguard FTSE All-Wld ex-US SmCp Idx	VSS	9%	5%	3%
WisdomTree International SmallCap Div	DLS	9%	6%	4%
Schwab Emerging Markets Equity	SCHE	9%	6%	4%
Vanguard Global ex-US Real Estate	VNQI	5%	3%	2%
iShares Barclays 1-3 Year Treasury Bond	SHY	0%	12%	18%
iShares Barclays 3-7 Year Treasury Bond	IEI	0%	20%	30%
iShares Barclays TIPS Bond	TIP	0%	8%	12%

ABOUT THE AUTHORS

Paul Merriman

Paul Merriman is nationally recognized as an authority on mutual funds, index investing, asset allocation and both buy-and-hold and active management strategies.

He is the founder of Paul A. Merriman & Associates, an investment advisory firm that is now Merriman LLC. The Seattle-based firm manages more than $1.5 billion for more than 2,000 households throughout the United States.

In his retirement, Paul remains passionately committed to educating and empowering investors. In 2012, he is working on the "How To Invest" series which distills his decades of expertise into concise investment books targeted to specific audiences.

Paul is also the author of four previous books on personal investing, including Financial Fitness Forever: 5 Steps To More Money, Less Risk and More Peace of Mind (McGraw Hill, Oct. 2011). The book was part of the "Financial Fitness Kit" offered on the TV show, "Financial Fitness After 50" that Paul created exclusively to raise funds for local Public

Broadcasting Service (PBS) stations. The kit also included a workbook, six CDs and five DVDs.

Paul's book, Live It Up Without Outliving Your Money! Creating The Perfect Retirement, published by John Wiley & Sons, was released in an updated edition June 2008.

Over the years Paul has led more than 1,000 investor workshops, hosted a weekly radio program and has been a featured guest on local, regional and national television shows. Paul has written many articles for FundAdvice..com, a service of Merriman LLC. This Web site was identified by Forbes as one of the best online resources for investors.

Paul's weekly podcast, "Sound Investing," was named by *Money* magazine as the best money podcast. Paul has been widely quoted in national publications and has spoken to many local chapters of the American Association of Individual Investors (AAII). Twice he has been a featured guest speaker at Harvard University's investor psychology conference.

Paul began his career in the 1960s, working briefly as a broker for a major Wall Street firm. He concluded that Wall Street was burdened with too many conflicts of interest and decided to help small companies raise venture capital. In 1979, he became president and chairman of a public manufacturing company in the Pacific Northwest. He retired in 1982 to create his independent investment management firm.

Paul is the recipient of a distinguished alumni award from Western Washington University's School of Economics and is a founding member of the board of directors of Global HELP, a Seattle-based non-profit organization that produces medical publications and distributes them free to doctors and other health care workers in developing nations.

Paul donates all profits from Regalo LLC to Global-Help and a scholarship fund at Western Washington University.

For questions and comments, Email: PM@PaulMerriman.com

Richard Buck

Richard Buck was a Seattle Times business reporter for 20 years, capping a 30-year journalism career that included eight years as a writer and editor for The Associated Press. He began working with Paul in 1993 and retired in the fall of 2011 as senior editor of Merriman Inc. In that position he helped Paul and other Merriman staff members write many articles and was the ghostwriter for Paul's previous books, Financial Fitness Forever and Live It Up Without Outliving Your Money! in addition to the How To Invest Series.

Richard has also chosen to receive no compensation and to donate all profits from the sale of this series to a scholarship fund at his alma mater, Willamette University.

Made in the USA
Monee, IL
21 May 2021